WEEKLY WRITING FOR THE MIDDLE GRADES

An Integrated Approach: Social Studies Themes

Jim McAlpine

Betty Weincek

Sue Jeweler

Marion Finkbinder

Educational Impressions

Text and Cover Illustrated by Karen Sigler

The purchase of this book entitles the individual teacher to reproduce copies of the student pages for use in his or her classroom exclusively. The reproduction of any part of the work for an entire school or school system or for commercial use is prohibited.

ISBN 1-56644-988-X

© 1996 Educational Impressions, Inc., Hawthorne, NJ

Printed in the U.S.A.

EDUCATIONAL IMPRESSIONS, INC.
Hawthorne, NJ 07507

TABLE OF CONTENTS

INTRODUCTION

Teachers in the "information age" are faced with challenges! So much to do...so little time. How can writing objectives, social studies objectives, and problem-solving objectives be taught along with reading, research, and language skills? There are not enough hours in the day.

But there is a way! Teachers can meet curricular and student performance requirements by clustering, telescoping, and/or combining objectives and outcomes between and across content areas.

For example, a teacher may be required to assess students on the following objectives:
- locate supporting evidence in information sources
- tell how one character attempts to persuade another character to do something
- list the causes of the Civil War
- write a friendly letter

An ideal activity combining these four "unconnected" objectives might be to:
Write a letter to your brother in which you are trying to persuade him to join you in the Confederate Army. In your persuasion, try to make your side's reasons for fighting seem more important and justifiable than the Union's.

From this one activity, a teacher can assess student mastery of the objectives given while offering each student the opportunity to be uniquely creative. Students master objectives in social studies, reading, research, language skills, and problem solving.

The demands of society will require students to integrate skills. This book is designed to give students experiences in dealing with factual information creatively at the higher levels of thinking – analysis, synthesis, and evaluation. These skills will transfer to other areas of learning and, most importantly, to real-life.

HOW TO USE THIS BOOK

1. Survey and cluster required curricular objectives

2. Determine which activities to use to address curricular requirements

3. Provide instruction on anticipated product outcomes

4. Decide on appropriate student groupings and/or organization

5. Make appropriate sheets available to students

6. Provide time for student research to address the first part of the activity

7. Provide closure for the research component

8. Provide directions and materials for the second component as an independent writing activity

9. Provide appropriate time for students to complete rough drafts for the independent writing activity

10. Provide students with opportunities to share, analyze, and refine the draft of the product

11. Determine the timeline for student submission of the product

12. Determine the evaluation form and format for student products

OBJECTIVES

Students will:

- use a variety of writing forms

- use factual information incorporating higher-order thinking skills (analysis, synthesis, evaluation)

- use research skills

- work creatively with information integrating content areas

- solve problems and perform tasks using real-life situations

AUDIENCE

Grades: 5-8

Content areas:

- American Studies
- World Studies
- English
- Reading
- Creative Writing
- Oral Communication
- Video Production
- Other

SIMULATION

The following are examples of students' responses to the Writing Activity: Write a ten-item Bill of Rights for stuffed animals. After a study of the United States BILL OF RIGHTS, students were given the activity sheets. The students understood the concept of the BILL OF RIGHTS and were able to creatively apply the concept to the writing assignment. Each student response was unique.

Sample Activity Sheet

BILL OF RIGHTS

BACKGROUND:
The United States Constitution, created in 1787, is the fundamental law of the land. It provides the basic framework for government. In 1791, ten changes, or amendments were added to the Constitution in order to protect the rights of citizens. These specified rights include freedom of the press, freedom of speech, freedom of religion, the right to a fair trial, and the right to bear arms.

WRITING ACTIVITY:
Write a ten-item Bill of Rights for stuffed animals.

TO ASSIST YOU:
• Find out about the Bill of Rights.
• Determine the categories of stuffed animals to be covered by your Bill of Rights.

Lisa Meck
5/31/95

Lions, Tigers, and Bears (OH, MY!) Bill of Rights

1.) Freedom from abuses by the little people, such as pulling tails, ripping off eyes, pushing noses in, and pulling off whiskers.

2.) The right to be kept clean and free of saliva, peanut butter, and tossed cookies.

3.) The right to be supervised and not to be left alone, or to be put back in normal area.

4.) The right not to be thrown in unpleasant places such as the toilet.

5.) The right to be loved, cuddled, and not thrown about.

6.) The right to bear arms, lion arms, and tiger arms.

7.) The right for the tag to stay on the animal, and not to be torn off.

8.) The right to be brought to trial by peers (only lions, tigers, and bears).

9.) The right not to be forgotten, and the right to be cared for.

10.) Just because the Bill of Rights (for stuffed animals) is for lions, tigers, and bears, other categories of stuffed animals cannot be denied their rights.

Tim Splain
June 1, 1995

The Teddy Bear
Bill of Rights

1. All Teddy Bears have the right to be considered not "just for babies" no matter what size, shape, or color the Teddy may be.

2. All Teddy Bears have the right to be hugged by their owners regularly.

3. All Teddy Bears have the right to be hugged exclusively by their owners and other family members. Only under written consent can a Teddy Bear be hugged by someone not meeting either of those requirements.

4. Teddy Bears have the right to the freedom of change. They may freely change size, shape, or color without a permit.

5. No Teddy Bear should be used as a weapon during a pillow fight.

6. If a Teddy Bear is caught in the middle of a pillow fight, it has the right to be immediately removed from the battleground and brought to a safe area.

7. All Teddy Bears have their medical needs taken care of by their owners. Torn off legs due to pillow fights must be carefully sewn back on.

8. All Teddy Bears have the right to be washed with special care with the special Bear Bounce softener. If the washing machine must be used, it should be turned onto the delicate cycle and the bear must be washed by itself.

9. All Teddy Bears must be remembered! No Teddy Bear should be left at Grandma's house, in the mall, in the museum, or in the backyard.

10. Teddy Bears have the right to charge any human who disobeys these laws (or makes them become disobeyed) with a public offense under the Stuffed Animal Rights Supreme Court.

Approved,

Timothy J. Splain
Stuffed Animal Rights President

Jonathan Wallace
June 1, 1995

Teddy Bear Amendments

I- The right to have a proper shelter.

II- The right to proper food, rest, and other care.

III- The right to a new owner after eight years of service.

IV- The right to "bear" arms; all Teddy bears must have functioning limbs.

V- The right to proper stuffing; all bears must be stuffed with pure cotton. No substitutes are permitted.

VI- Right to worship former President Theodore Roosevelt; this god may be worshipped as an option.

VII- The right to have any color of fur; however, teddy bears are not to be judged by the color of their fur.

VIII- The right to a "junk-free" stomach; nothing should be put into the bear's stomach without the bear's consent.

IX- The right to bar humans from their sacred "Teddy Bear Picnic."

X- Other rights may be applied in different households. These amendments on this bill are in effect but more may be added.

Catrin Darsley
May 31, 1995

Bill of Rights

We, the toys, demanded a Bill of Rights.

As usual, we got what we wanted. Here is our own Bill of Rights.

1. Every stuffed toy is entitled to periodic washes at least once every six months.

2. Every stuffed toy is entitled to at least two combings per month, clean clothing (or fur), a genial, kind owner, and a clean, neat, warm home.

3. No creature shall have the right to beat the stuffing out of any toy.

4. No creature may squash, marmalize, mutilate, or pull off any of a toy's clothing or body parts.

5. All toys have equal rights.

6. It is guaranteed that all toys have the freedom of speech, freedom of the fourth estate, etc.

7. Every toy is entitled to a fair trial and the right to sue the judge and jury.

8. No toy is to be thrown into the air against his own will.

WEEKLY
WRITING ACTIVITIES

EXPLORATION

BACKGROUND:
The Renaissance was a time for the "rebirth" of learning. New ideas and inventions contributed to the Age of Exploration and Discovery. Along with trade in the Middle East and the increase of political power and wealth among the European countries, exploration flourished. Early European explorers to North America were Bjarni Herjulfsson and Leif Ericsson. Great explorations funded by the Spanish, Dutch, Portuguese, French, and English occurred during the sixteenth and seventeenth centuries. Explorers included Marco Polo, Magellan, Cortés, Columbus, Pizarro, Cabot, Drake, Hudson, Cartier, and Joliet.

WRITING ACTIVITY:
Create a Venn diagram which compares/contrasts two explorers.

TO ASSIST YOU:
• Determine how a Venn diagram is used.
• Research each explorer.

Write a Biographical Piece
Based on a Venn Diagram...

You are a biographer. Your publisher is creating an anthology of famous explorers. You have been given the option of writing a biographical piece that discusses either the similarities of two explorers or their differences.

Make your decision as to the focus of the piece. After deciding on the focus, write a biographical piece based on the Venn diagram information.

On this page, begin a draft of your biographical piece.

_____

_____

_____

_____

_____

_____

_____

_____

_____

_____

_____

_____

Share your draft with a partner. Make changes based upon suggestions. Proofread very carefully.

On a separate piece of paper, write the final copy of your piece based upon the Venn diagram.

PRINCE HENRY THE NAVIGATOR

BACKGROUND:
Prince Henry the Navigator (1394-1460) of Portugal encouraged and promoted exploration of the west coast of Africa during the 1400s. While he never went on any of the voyages he sponsored, he sent out more than fifty such expeditions to find a water route to the trade riches of the East. As a result of his encouragement, Portugal became the leader among European nations of the time in navigational skills and gained large colonial holdings in Africa. In 1441, one of Henry's expeditions brought back to Europe the first Africans to arrive as slaves. In the fifty years after Henry's death, the knowledge obtained because of his support of new navigational tools and thinking enabled Europeans to literally sail around the world and to discover what they called the New World.

WRITING ACTIVITY:
As Prince Henry, develop a plan/procedure for encouraging more exploration. Your plan/procedure should include motivation, rationale, rewards, and a sequence of events.

TO ASSIST YOU:
• Research procedural plan.
• Research rationale, motivation, etc. for exploration in Henry's time.
• Research lifestyles and culture of the time.

Write a Plan/Procedure...

You are director of the Woods Hole Oceanographic Institution, a private, non-profit research center for marine science on Cape Cod, at Woods Hole, Massachusetts.

You are to develop a plan/procedure for encouraging the exploration of the ocean's floor today.

On this page, begin a draft for your plan/procedure.

_____

_____

_____

_____

_____

_____

_____

_____

_____

_____

_____

_____

_____

Share your draft with a partner. Make changes based upon suggestions. Proofread very carefully.

On a separate sheet of paper, write the final copy of your plan/procedure for encouraging the exploration of the ocean's floor.

HORSES

BACKGROUND:

Horses roamed across the Western Hemisphere approximately 10,000 years ago. Mysteriously, they disappeared. Horses were domesticated and widely used in the Eastern Hemisphere, where they had continued to develop. Columbus returned horses to the New World when he brought several to the Caribbean island of Hispaniola on his voyage of 1494. The Spaniards continued to bring horses to the New World, and by 1500 horses could be found in Cuba and Central America. Hernando Cortés transported sixteen horses from Cuba to Mexico in 1519. The Aztecs were awed by the force and the frightening power of the unknown animal. Consequently, a small number of Spaniards were able to conquer the civilization of Mexico. Horses eventually became an important part of many tribal groups who trained, traded, and used them. The animals were used for hunting, as draft animals for farming, and for travel. Horses changed the lives of the Native Americans in North, South, and Central America.

WRITING ACTIVITY:

Write a lecture for a history teacher to use in order to explain the impact of the horse on the Aztecs as a "metaphor" for the impact of the tank on modern warfare.

OR

Write a lecture for a history teacher to use in order to explain the impact of the horse by tribal groups as a "metaphor" for the impact of the internal combustion engine on transportation and farming.

TO ASSIST YOU:
• Explain a metaphor.
• Research the use of horses in warfare.
• Research the use of the horse in transportation and farming.
• Research the invention and use of tanks.
• Research the invention of the internal combustion engine.

Write a Poem...

You are the Poet Laureate of the United Nations.

Create a verse which uses the rise and fall of the use of the horse in warfare.

On this page, begin a draft of your verse.

_____

_____

_____

_____

_____

_____

_____

_____

_____

_____

_____

_____

_____

_____

Share your draft with a partner. Make changes based upon suggestions. Proofread very carefully.

On a separate sheet of paper, write the final copy of your poem based upon the horse lecture.

19

COLONIZATION

BACKGROUND:
Explorers to the New World brought back to Europe wonderful stories about the potential wealth which could be taken from their discoveries. These stories, coupled with social, political, economic, and religious troubles in Europe, made colonization and the settlement of land in North America attractive enough to become possible. At first, small groups of Europeans traveled by ship and started colonies such as Jamestown in Virginia and Plymouth in Massachusetts. As the settlements prospered, new waves of immigrants followed. By 1733, thirteen British colonies were established along the eastern coast. The French had settled along the St. Lawrence and Mississippi Rivers and the Spanish in Central and South America and along the west coast.

WRITING ACTIVITY:
Write a science-fiction story about colonization.

TO ASSIST YOU:
• Find out about science fiction as a writing style.
• Find out about colonization in general and the colonies in America in particular.

Write a Storyboard...

You have been hired by Steven Spielberg to transcribe the science-fiction story on colonization into a cartoon feature film.

Create a storyboard for presentation to Mr. Spielberg at a first developmental meeting.

On this page, begin a draft of your storyboard.

Share your draft with a partner. Make changes based upon suggestions. Proofread very carefully.

On a separate piece of paper, write the final copy of your storyboard based upon the science-fiction story on colonization.

BILL OF RIGHTS

BACKGROUND:
The United States Constitution, created in 1787, is the fundamental law of the land. It provides the basic framework for government. In 1791, ten changes, or amendments, were added to the Constitution in order to protect the rights of citizens. These specified rights include freedom of the press, freedom of speech, freedom of religion, the right to a fair trial, and the right to bear arms.

WRITING ACTIVITY:
Write a ten-item Bill of Rights for stuffed animals.

TO ASSIST YOU:
• Find out about the Bill of Rights.
• Determine the categories of stuffed animals to be covered by your Bill of Rights.

Write a Speech...

You are a teddy bear. You believe that your stuffed-animal rights have been violated by a human.

Write and deliver a speech to the Stuffed-Animal Rights Supreme Court pleading your case.

On this page, begin a draft of your speech.

_____

_____

_____

_____

_____

_____

_____

_____

_____

_____

_____

_____

Share your draft with a partner. Make changes based upon suggestions. Proofread very carefully.

On a separate sheet of paper, write the final copy of your speech based upon your Bill of Rights for stuffed animals.

THE TRAIL OF TEARS

BACKGROUND:
President Andrew Jackson insisted that Native Americans be removed to lands west of the Mississippi River because settlers wanted to use the rich, fertile land for farming. The Indian Removal Act of 1830 was passed by Congress. All surviving Native Americans east of the Mississippi, including the Cherokee, Chicksaw, Choctaw, Creek, and Seminole, among others, were forced to leave their land to live in a new territory known today as Oklahoma. Jackson sent the army to force the Native Americans out. Although some tribes resisted, it was an impossible task against army guns and troops. Approximately one fourth of the Native Americans died on the trail during the winter of 1838 from cold, hunger, and disease. This march has been called the "Trail of Tears."

WRITING ACTIVITY:
You are a journalist working for a liberal eastern newspaper at the time of the implementation of the Indian Removal Act. You have been assigned to write a series of articles about the relocation of the native peoples. In your articles, you decide to record and use the people's laments about their journey. Write one newspaper article about the impact of the beginning of the journey; another about the strain of the journey itself; and a third article about the reactions to and impact of the resettlement site in Oklahoma.

TO ASSIST YOU:
• Research the Native Americans' description of the "Trail of Tears."
• Identify the viewpoint which would have been held by a "liberal" newspaper.
• Find out about the physical, economic, and environmental conditions of the lands at both ends of the "Trail of Tears."

Write a Critique...

You are a descendant of one of the Native Americans who experienced the "Trail of Tears." You have discovered the articles written by a journalist from the 1830s.

Based upon your knowledge and understanding of your people, critique the effectiveness and efficiency this reporter used in recording your people's experience.

On this page, begin a draft of your critique.

_____

_____

_____

_____

_____

_____

_____

_____

_____

_____

_____

_____

Share your draft with a partner. Make changes based upon suggestions. Proofread very carefully.

On a separate sheet of paper, write the final copy of your critique based upon the reporter's articles.

THE GOLD RUSH

BACKGROUND:

Johann Sutter, a Swiss immigrant, settled in the Sacramento River Valley in California and built a cattle ranch and tannery. In 1848, James Marshall, who was at work building a water-powered sawmill for Sutter, found gold on the property. By 1849, the California Trail was crowded with "forty-niners" heading west to "strike it rich." Over ninety thousand people traveled the overland route or came by water around Cape Horn in hopes of finding gold. The Gold Rush stimulated the building of clipper ships and contributed to the rapid settlement of the west.

WRITING ACTIVITY:

Create a series of newspaper and broadside advertisements for a competition between "overland" versus "around the Horn" transportation to the gold fields of California.

TO ASSIST YOU:

• Find out about the overland and water routes to California.
• Find out about the hardships inherent in each route.
• Research the design and intent of newspapers and broadside ads of the time.

Write a Letter...

You are a young person with "gold fever." You are being bombarded by ads for various ways to get to California.

Write a friendly letter to your mom eleviating her fears about your journey west. Explain why your choice is the least dangerous.

On this page, begin a draft for your letter.

_____

_____

_____

_____

_____

_____

_____

_____

_____

_____

_____

Share your draft with a partner. Make changes based upon suggestions. Proofread very carefully.

On a separate sheet of paper, write the final copy of your letter based upon the California advertisements.

SOJOURNER TRUTH

BACKGROUND:

Sojourner Truth (1797?-1883) was the name used by the first black woman orator to speak out publicly against slavery. Her real name was Isabella Baumfree. Born a slave, she was freed in 1827. By 1843 she believed that God had given her the charge to speak out against slavery. She took the name Sojourner Truth while travelling throughout New England and the midwest speaking and lecturing, first about the love of God and concern for her fellow man, and later in favor of abolishing slavery. In 1864, she met with President Lincoln in Washington, D.C., where she stayed to work for the betterment of blacks. She also lobbied Congress after the Civil War to reserve undeveloped lands in the west for farms for blacks. This proposal did not get government support.

WRITING ACTIVITY:

As a United States senator who was a friend of Sojourner Truth and who supported her proposal regarding western lands, write a letter to Sojourner explaining how and why the idea failed.

TO ASSIST YOU:

• Research events, social, and cultural conditions of the times in the United States.
• Research living conditions of the times.
• Research the components of a persuasive speech.

Write a Speech...

You are Sojourner Truth.

Write a speech to be given in the Congress of the United States to help lobby support for the cause of your proposal regarding western lands for blacks.

On this page begin a draft of your speech.

_____

_____

_____

_____

_____

_____

_____

_____

_____

_____

_____

_____

_____

Share your draft with a partner. Make changes based upon suggestions. Proofread very carefully.

On a separate sheet of paper, write the final copy of your speech based upon Sojourner Truth's proposal.

RECONSTRUCTION

BACKGROUND:

The period following the American Civil War, from 1865-1877, is known as Reconstruction. At that time, the goals of the government were to reconstitute relations between the Union and Confederate states, rebuild the war-torn South, and provide laws protecting the rights of freed slaves. Many controversies developed during this period. There was heated debate over the criteria for readmission of Confederate states into the Union. Southern whites had difficulty accepting black equality. Southern governments lacked the financial support to recover economically. Lincoln's assassination occurred one week after the end of the Civil War. Although Lincoln had established a Reconstruction plan, the new President, Andrew Johnson, wanted to use his own program. In both programs, slavery was to be abolished, but Johnson's allowed for no specific role for blacks. Efforts were made to eliminate Southern white control. The thirteenth and fourteenth Amendments to the U.S. Constitution were ratified by Congress, the Civil Rights Act was passed, and the Freedmen's Bureau was established to build schools, hospitals, and jobs for freed slaves. Southern whites, however, gained control of state governments. They developed Black Codes, which regulated and limited black involvement in business, voting, and land ownership. Groups like the Ku Klux Klan formed to oppose equality for blacks, and violent racial attacks became the norm. It wasn't until the second half of the twentieth century that blacks began to be granted the rights bequeathed to them during Reconstruction.

WRITING ACTIVITY:

Create a crossword puzzle for an American history class attending school in the 1870s. The crossword puzzle must include as many words related to the Reconstruction period as possible. The crossword puzzle grid must be square and no smaller than ten spaces by ten spaces and no longer than twenty spaces by twenty spaces.

TO ASSIST YOU:

• Compile a list of words and clues related to Reconstruction.
• Find out about crossword puzzle construction.

Create a Crossword Puzzle...

It is one hundred and twenty years **after** Reconstruction.

You are to create a crossword puzzle related to contemporary civil rights. In your puzzle you are to use current words **and** include as many words from the Reconstruction period that are still applicable.

OR

Use the 1870s crossword puzzle grid. Reword the clues to fit the years 1965 to the present.

On this page, begin a draft of your crossword puzzle.

Share your draft with a partner. Make changes based upon suggestions. Proofread very carefully.

On a separate sheet of paper, write the final copy of your crossword puzzle based upon the Reconstruction puzzle.

INDUSTRIAL REVOLUTION

BACKGROUND:

The American Industrial Revolution took place during the nineteenth century. Tremendous growth in business and technology occurred. Machines replaced hand tools, and factories hired men, women, and children for six-day work weeks and 18-hour days. Many worked for $2.00 per week or less. The first textile mill was built in Pawtucket, Rhode Island. Steel, created by the Bessemer process, was being turned out by factories in 1865. Inventions and improvements in machinery made factory life the dominant way of living for the poor. The newest immigrants from Ireland, Wales, and Germany became the labor force.

WRITING ACTIVITY:

The year is 1901. Write a persuasive speech for a banker or investor to deliver. The speech is intended to support investment in the building of new factories.

TO ASSIST YOU:
• Determine the audience for the speech.
• Research the role of investors in the Industrial Revolution.
• Research the benefits and short-comings of the new factory construction.
• Assess the labor requirements for a new factory.

Create a Rallying Song...

You are an organizer of the opposition to more factory development. Your opposition is based on overcrowding, poor housing, pollution, etc. You have heard the speech.

You are to write a rallying song to unite the masses against the factories and the owners.

On this page, begin a draft for your rallying song.

_____

_____

_____

_____

_____

_____

_____

_____

_____

_____

_____

_____

_____

_____

Share your draft with a partner. Make changes based upon suggestions. Proofread very carefully.

On a separate sheet of paper, write the final copy of your rallying song based upon the investor's persuasive speech.

INVENTIONS

BACKGROUND:
Inventions are new products, processes, and ideas that did not previously exist. They provide a more effective and/or efficient way to do something. People invent things to fill a need. For example, the light bulb was developed to increase the productivity of factories. With light bulbs, factories could be operated without natural light, making them usable twenty-four hours a day. Inventors sometimes create products when there is no need; therefore, they must create a need. For example, nobody really needed seasonal flags to fly in their yards, but when seasonal flags were invented and marketed, many people wanted one. It is hard to tell if the old saying, "Necessity is the mother of invention," is more or less true if written, "Invention is the mother of necessity." Perhaps both are true.

WRITING ACTIVITY:
Prepare the argument for a debate on the merits of the issue "Necessity is the mother of invention" or "Invention is the mother of necessity."

TO ASSIST YOU:
• Find out about the process for preparing for a debate.
• Define the term "conundrum."

Write a Marketing Plan...

You are a chemist who has accidentally made a material that is non-toxic and flexible and which has all the properties of both cloth and plastic.

Develop a need for this invention by creating a comprehensive marketing plan.

On this page, begin a draft of your marketing plan.

_____

_____

_____

_____

_____

_____

_____

_____

_____

_____

_____

_____

_____

Share your draft with a partner. Make changes based upon suggestions. Proofread very carefully.

On a separate sheet of paper, write the final copy of your marketing plan based upon your argument about the conundrum.

EUROPEAN IMMIGRATION TO THE UNITED STATES IN THE LATE NINETEENTH AND EARLY TWENTIETH CENTURIES

BACKGROUND:

Immigrants are people who came from one country to live in another country. Between the end of the Civil War and the beginning of World War I more than 12 million people emigrated from Europe to the United States. These people traveled in steerage class aboard steamships. Steerage passage could be purchased for as little as $10.00. They were often squeezed together in the bottom of the ship where conditions were terrible. Upon arrival in the United States, the immigrants had to face rigorous screening for health, appearance, and economic potential.

WRITING ACTIVITY:

As a person your age in the time of the great tide of immigration in the late nineteenth and early twentieth centuries, write a journal of your travels from your homeland to your arrival in the United States. Include each step of your journey from your home, to the place of embarkation on a ship, the transatlantic crossing, and your final destination. Be sure to include the location of your homeland, reasons for leaving, personal reactions, feelings and emotions, and dates which would match the reality of such an adventure.

TO ASSIST YOU:
• Find out about the conditions of steerage class for immigrants.
• Find out about reasons for immigrating.
• Find out about conditions in the region of your choice in Europe in the late nineteenth century.
• Find out about conditions and procedures for new immigrant arrivals.

Performance-Based Assessments

You have discovered a journal of a European immigrant in your attic. You know that this immigrant was about your age when he/she wrote his/her journal. You are delighted by your find because you now have something to submit for a family-reunion yearbook.

You arc to write a biographical sketch about the writer of the journal. Your sketch is to be no longer than one page.

On this page, begin a draft for your biographical sketch.

_____

_____

_____

_____

_____

_____

_____

_____

_____

_____

_____

_____

Share your draft with a partner. Make changes based upon suggestions. Proofread very carefully.

On a separate sheet of paper, write the final copy of your biographical sketch based upon the journal information.

CITIES

BACKGROUND:

Cities developed when and where enough food and wealth had accumulated for people to stay in one place. This wealth made it possible for these people to trade for or buy the things they needed like food, goods, and services. As more people gathered and became specialists in a variety of areas, farming around the new city increased as did trade within and throughout the city. In the past, cities grew where trade routes crossed or at or near the mouths of rivers. In more recent times, cities have been founded where people decided they wanted or needed them. Technology made it possible to bring food and services to the site. Older cities like Cairo, Shanghai, London, and Calcutta began in the traditional way. Newer cities like Brasilia, Washington, D.C., Los Angeles, and New Delhi are located where people decided to place them.

WRITING ACTIVITY:

Write a plan defending your choice for the site of the new capital of the world.

TO ASSIST YOU:

• Examine a map of the world.
• Decide on what is necessary for the site of a world capital.
• Determine the political/economic/social/technological/geographic necessities for selecting the world capital site.

Write an Explanation...

You are the Secretary General of the United Nations.

Develop and explain how the new site for the world capital will be determined and implemented.

On this page, begin a draft of your explanation.

_____

_____

_____

_____

_____

_____

_____

_____

_____

_____

_____

_____

_____

Share your draft with a partner. Make changes based upon suggestions. Proofread very carefully.

On a separate sheet of paper, write the final copy of your explanation based upon the plan.

CANADA AND BRITISH RULE

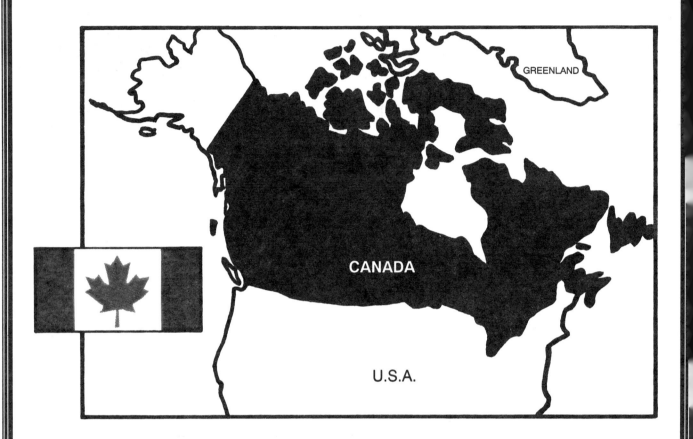

BACKGROUND:

The Quebec Act of 1774 was passed by the British Parliament. The law made it possible for French Canadians to practice their own religion, keep their existing laws, and speak French. After the American Revolution, Britain was concerned about a similar Canadian revolution. It did not occur. In 1867, the British North American Act united all of Canada into one nation and made Canada a representative government. By 1931, Canada, under the Statute of Westminster, conducted its own foreign affairs. Today, Canada is a member of the Commonwealth of Nations and remains a territory that gives allegiance to Britain.

WRITING ACTIVITY:

Write an essay in which you objectively present the positives and negatives of Canada functioning as a bilingual nation.

TO ASSIST YOU:

• Identify the major language groups of Canada.
• Find out about bilingualism.
• Find out about the causes of language regionalism in Canada.

Write a Speech...

You are a member of the United States Congress and you are going to use points made in the essay regarding bilingualism in Canada to support or refute the move toward an official national language for the United States.

Write your speech for the next session of Congress.

OR

Debate the same question for any other country.

On this page, begin a draft of your speech.

_____

_____

_____

_____

_____

_____

_____

_____

_____

_____

_____

_____

Share your draft with a partner. Make changes based upon suggestions. Proofread very carefully.

On a separate sheet of paper, write the final copy of your speech based upon the essay.

MEXICO: CINCO de MAYO

BACKGROUND:

In 1810, the Mexican people united in revolt against Spanish rule and finally won their independence from Spain in 1821. Independence, however, failed to solve many of Mexico's problems. Benito Juarez, who became president in 1857, did the most to create change. Owing money to Britain, Spain, and France, Juarez told the nations that the debt could not be paid back for years. France decided to invade Mexico. On May 5, 1862, a small band of Mexicans defeated the larger French army. This battle is celebrated today as Cinco de Mayo, Mexico's national holiday commemorating the French defeat. The French were finally driven off Mexican soil in 1867, and Juarez served as president until he died in 1872.

WRITING ACTIVITY:
Write the resumé of Benito Juarez.

TO ASSIST YOU:
• Determine the components of a resumé.
• Research the entire life of Benito Juarez.

Create a Poster...

You are a graphic artist in the public relations office of the Mexican government. Your job has been to design a poster about Juarez for a Cinco de Mayo celebration in Mexico City.

Create a poster which includes graphic design and appropriate copy.

On this page, begin a draft of your poster.

Share your draft with a partner. Make changes based upon suggestions. Proofread very carefully.

On a separate sheet of paper, create the final copy of your poster based upon the resumé of Benito Juarez.

THE RENAISSANCE

Desiderius Erasmus (1466-1536)

BACKGROUND:
The Renaissance, or the "revival of learning," signaled the end of the Middle Ages in western Europe. During the fifteenth and sixteenth centuries in Italy, there was a renewal of interest and curiosity about science, art, and nature. As wealth increased, new ideas and inventions spread across Europe making voyages of discovery, the spread of literature, and the pursuit of knowledge possible. Erasmus, Leonardo da Vinci, Michelangelo, Petrarch, Shakespeare, and Raphael were some of the great figures of the time.

WRITING ACTIVITY:
Develop a recipe for creating the Renaissance.
OR
Develop a recipe for creating a Renaissance.

TO ASSIST YOU:
• Identify all the necessary ingredients for a Renaissance.
• Identify/hypothesize the sequencing of combining the ingredients of a Renaissance.
• Consider unique variables for a Renaissance in different areas.
• Decide on the importance of amounts/quantities of the ingredients.
• Decide the specific area or place in history for which you are developing your Renaissance recipe.

Write an Editorial...

You are a mayor of a depressed urban center. You have determined that the recipe for a Renaissance can be applied to your city.

Write an editorial for your city's Sunday paper in which you present the recipe for your city's Renaissance and the specific elements to be included.

On this page, begin a draft for your editorial.

_____

_____

_____

_____

_____

_____

_____

_____

_____

_____

_____

_____

Share your draft with a partner. Make changes based upon suggestions. Proofread very carefully.

On a separate sheet of paper, write the final copy of your editorial based upon the Renaissance recipe.

THE FERTILE CRESCENT

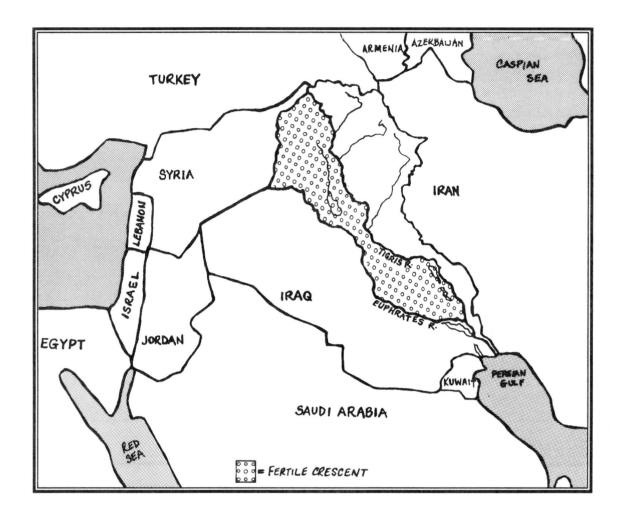

BACKGROUND:
The crescent-shaped land, located in Asia from the Mediterranean Sea to the Persian Gulf in the valley between the Tigris and Euphrates Rivers, is said to be the birthplace of one of the first civilizations. More than 5,000 years ago, the Sumerians chose to develop this area because of its rich soil, which was suitable for farming. Later civilizations such as Babylonia, Assyria, and Phoenicia began here also.

WRITING ACTIVITY:
Create a brochure to publicize the availability of "dig" sites in the Fertile Crescent for professional and advanced amateur archaeologists.

TO ASSIST YOU:
• Determine the structure, purpose, and format of the brochure.
• Identify what archaeologists do and how they do it.
• Find out about civilizations known to have existed in the Fertile Crescent.
• Find out about the potential finds for archaeologists.

Write an Abstract...
Write a Business Letter...

You are an archaeologist who has just returned from a "dig" in the Fertile Crescent.

Write an abstract describing your finds. Develop your theory and explain the structure of the civilization.

OR

You are an archaeologist who has received the brochure and you want to go, but you do not have any funding.

Write a business letter to the Ford Foundation requesting money to assist you in this pursuit. Be sure to include information provided by the brochure.

On this page, begin your draft of your abstract or business letter.

_____

_____

_____

_____

_____

_____

_____

_____

_____

Share your draft with a partner. Make changes based upon suggestions. Proofread very carefully.

On a separate sheet of paper, write the final copy of your abstract or business letter based upon the brochure.

PYRAMIDS

BACKGROUND:

Pyramids, the gigantic tombs for Egyptian pharoahs, were constructed between 3000 and 2500 B.C. The largest of the three monumental tombs at Giza, the Great Pyramid, was built by Khufu for his own burial and entry into the afterlife. It is believed that it took at least twenty years to complete and that it was built by at least 100,000 slaves. The interior of pyramids included furnished burial chambers, small rooms used by priests, false doors, and passages constructed to mislead tomb robbers. These efforts were futile because the three major pyramids were looted long before the modern era.

WRITING ACTIVITY:

Create a set of decodable glyphs which give directions for the high priests to exit the pyramid after the burial of the pharoah.

TO ASSIST YOU:
• Research glyphs.
• Research pyramid construction.

Write a Monograph...

You are a modern-day archaeologist.

You are to write a monograph on the messages that have been left as graffiti on the pyramids over the centuries.

On this page, begin a draft for your monograph.

_____

_____

_____

_____

_____

_____

_____

_____

_____

_____

_____

_____

Share your draft with a partner. Make changes based upon suggestions. Proofread very carefully.

On a separate sheet of paper, write the final copy of your monograph based upon the Egyptian glyphs.

CLEOPATRA

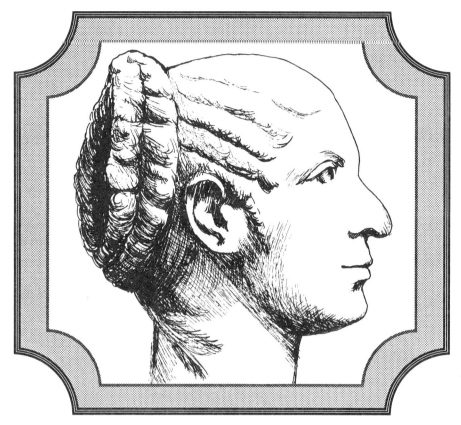

BACKGROUND:

Cleopatra (69-30 B.C.) was queen of Egypt from 51 B.C. until her death. She became queen, or co-ruler, of Egypt after the death of her father and her marriage to her brother, Ptolemy XIII. Ptolemy was deposed by his guardians, and Cleopatra was banished. She returned as queen after the death of Ptolemy XIII and the defeat of her enemies by Julius Caesar and a Roman army. She fell in love with Caesar and had her younger brother, Ptolemy XIV, who was now her husband, killed so that she and her son by Caesar could rule Egypt. Caesar was murdered in Rome while she was there. A few years later Cleopatra fell in love with Mark Antony. She wanted her children by Caesar or Antony to become the next in line to rule Rome. When Antony and Octavian were in a civil war over who should rule Rome, rumors spread that Cleopatra had committed suicide. Antony stabbed himself in grief. Unable to reach an agreement with Octavian regarding peace and the future rights of her children, Cleopatra killed herself by allowing an asp, a poisonous snake, to bite her.

WRITING ACTIVITY:

As a stand-up comic, write five jokes or funny riddles about Cleopatra's life.

TO ASSIST YOU:
• Research Cleopatra.
• Identify the elements of jokes.
• Identify the elements of riddles.

Write a Limerick or Clerihew...

You are Cleopatra's fool. You must create a limerick or clerihew about Cleopatra which will not get you beheaded.

Write a limerick or clerihew.

On this page, begin a draft for your limerick or clerihew.

_____

_____

_____

_____

_____

_____

_____

_____

_____

_____

_____

_____

_____

Share your draft with a partner. Make changes based upon suggestions. Proofread very carefully.

On a separate sheet of paper, write the final copy of your limerick or clerihew.

ALEXANDER THE GREAT

BACKGROUND:

Alexander the Great (356-323 B.C.) was one of history's greatest generals. At twenty, he became king of the Macedonians after the murder of his father, Philip II, by one of Philip's bodyguards. Alexander brought Greece, Asia Minor, most of the Mediterranean basin, and even part of India under Macedonian control and influence. By doing so, he spread the Hellenistic culture and created the so-called Golden Age of Greek history.

WRITING ACTIVITY:

Create an autobiography which Alexander had been in the process of writing. This document has been found in his supposed tomb. In it, he wrote about and commented on his life and accomplishments. It begins with his earliest memories about home life and continues until just before his death.

TO ASSIST YOU:

• Find a timeline of Alexander's life and accomplishments.
• Locate information on the Hellenistic period.
• Research the size, scope, and sequence of the development of the Empire.

Write a Tall Tale...

You are a storyteller

You want to preserve the story of Alexander the Great's life and accomplishments, so you create an original tall tale.

On this page, begin a draft of your tall tale.

_____

_____

_____

_____

_____

_____

_____

_____

_____

_____

_____

_____

_____

Share your draft with a partner. Make changes based upon suggestions. Proofread very carefully.

On a separate sheet of paper, write the final copy of your tall tale based upon the autobiography of Alexander the Great.

GREEK THEATRE

BACKGROUND:

Ancient Greek comedy and tragedy combined song, language, and meter with oration, dance, and ceremonial group movement. The dramas were an educational force on the spectators. The plays were intended to stir the emotions of love, fear, pity, anger, excitement, pleasure, sorrow, and sometimes loathing in playgoers. Greek playwrights included Sophocles, Euripedes, Aeschylus, and Aristophanes. Many of today's theatrical techniques were introduced and used by the Greeks of the fifth century B.C.

WRITING ACTIVITY:

Choose a contemporary television show. Rewrite the script for this TV show into the form of Greek theatre.
OR
Choose a Greek play. Rewrite it into a thirty-minute television script.

TO ASSIST YOU:
- Identify elements of Greek theatre.
- Identify elements of a TV show.
- Determine casting, set requirements, costumes, and other technical components.
- Determine scripting requirements to transcribe between two media.

Write a Proposal...

You have decided to submit your script to a local theatre group for production. Their requirement is that all plays must fit the form and format of classic Greek theatre.

Write a proposal supporting your own play in which you explain how and why it fits the requirements of the theatre group. Your proposal is to be no longer than one page.

On this page, begin a draft of your proposal.

_____

_____

_____

_____

_____

_____

_____

_____

_____

_____

_____

_____

_____

Share your draft with a partner. Make changes based upon suggestions. Proofread carefully.

On a separate sheet of paper, write the final copy of your proposal based upon the script.

ROMAN ARCHITECTURE

BACKGROUND:

As a result of prosperity, vast trading, and large population growth during the Roman Empire, which began in 27 B.C. and lasted 500 years, the building of large public structures grew and developed into a distinctive style. This architectural change occurred as a result of several innovations: concrete vaulting, the rounded arch, and the organization of capital and labor to expedite the construction of these large projects. Concrete and brick were used by Nero to rebuild the city around his palace after the famous fire. Structures built included utility structures, public baths, arenas, apartment houses, and temples. Often, rooms in these buildings were designed using various geometric shapes, corridors, staircases, and recesses. Roman architecture is acclaimed more for its structural components than for ornamentation because the Romans copied the Greek techniques for decoration. Once the rebuilding process and style were perfected, both spread and were imitated and replicated throughout the Empire.

WRITING ACTIVITY:

Write a glossary of terms used and applied to Roman style architecture.

TO ASSIST YOU:

• Determine the elements of a glossary.
• Research Roman architecture.
• Research Romanesque architecture.
• Research Greek architecture.

Write a Word Picture...

You are an architect. Design a Romanesque style villa.

Describe this villa as a word picture for a blind student in an architecture appreciation course.

On this page, begin a draft of your word picture.

_____

_____

_____

_____

_____

_____

_____

_____

_____

_____

_____

_____

_____

Share your draft with a partner. Make changes based upon suggestions. Proofread very carefully.

On a separate piece of paper, write the final copy of your word picture based upon the glossary of terms.

THE GREAT WALL OF CHINA

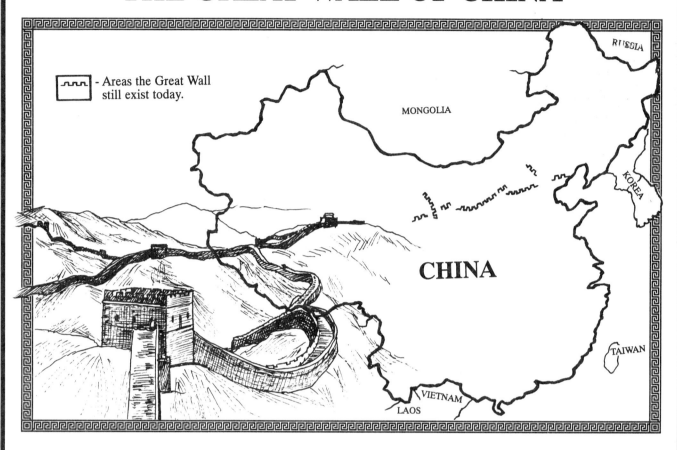

- Areas the Great Wall still exist today.

RUSSIA

MONGOLIA

KOREA

CHINA

TAIWAN

VIETNAM

LAOS

BACKGROUND:

The Great Wall of China is the world's longest man-made structure. It was built by hand over a period of time from the 600s B.C. through the 1400s A.D. Though it was not built as one piece, its purpose was to protect China from invasion from the north. Because of this, its several smaller sections were finally joined into an approximately 4,000-mile-long (6,400-km) structure. The wall crosses mountains, rivers, and valleys following the contour of the land and is thought by some Chinese to resemble a dragon protecting their homeland. Large portions of the wall consist of a causeway connecting watchtowers every 100 to 200 yards (91 to 180 meters) apart. The causeway is up to 35 feet (11 meters) above the ground and can be as wide as twenty feet (6 meters) in places where the base of the wall is about 25 feet (7.6 meters) wide. Over the centuries, sections of the wall have fallen into ruin, and an extensive restoration program has been ongoing since 1949. Today the Great Wall of China does not keep invaders out, but attracts them as tourists.

WRITING ACTIVITY:

Write a song lyric in which the dragon is a metaphor for the Great Wall and its role and troubles throughout history.

TO ASSIST YOU:

• Find out about the role of the dragon in Chinese culture and mythology.
• Find out about metaphors.

Write a Myth...

You are a writer of children's books for a major publisher in China.

Create a present-day myth to explain the role of the Great Wall in Communist China.

On this page, begin a draft of your myth.

_____

_____

_____

_____

_____

_____

_____

_____

_____

_____

_____

_____

_____

_____

Share your draft with a partner. Make changes based upon suggestions. Proofread very carefully.

On a separate sheet of paper, write the final copy of your myth.

BUDDHA

BACKGROUND:
Gautama is considered the founder of what has come to be called Buddhism. It is believed that he was born in India 560 years before Jesus and was a prince of Nepal. Sitting under a Bo-tree, Buddha, the "enlightened one," understood the meaning of life. For the remaining years of his life, he traveled throughout India with his disciples, preaching his views. Buddhism, a religion of eastern and central Asia, grew out of Gautama's teachings. He taught that suffering is inherent in life and that a person can be liberated from it by moral self-purification.

WRITING ACTIVITY:
Transcribe the basic tenets of Buddhism into contemporary language.

TO ASSIST YOU:
• Research Buddhism.
• Use a thesaurus.

Create a Game with Written Directions...

You are a game designer.

Create a game with written directions using Buddhist tenets for which the objective or "object of the game" is to reach Nirvana.

On this page, begin a draft of your game and directions.

_____

_____

_____

_____

_____

_____

_____

_____

_____

_____

_____

_____

_____

Share your draft with a partner. Make changes based upon suggestions. Proofread very carefully.

On a separate sheet of paper, write the final copy of your game and directions based upon the tenets of Buddhism.

THE SILK ROAD

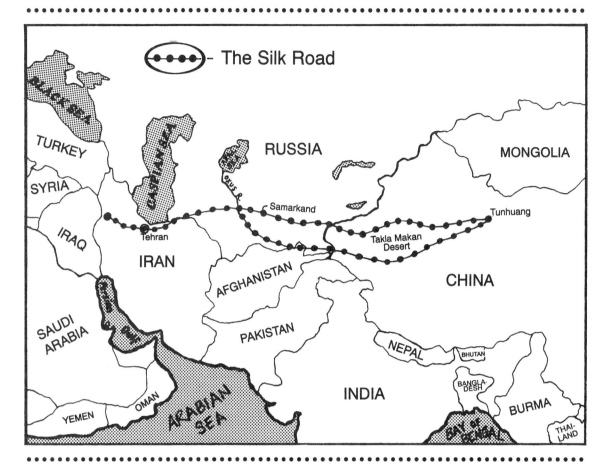

BACKGROUND:

The Silk Road was a trade route for caravans opened by the emperors of the Kushan Empire of northwestern India (A.D. 50-200) to link China with India and the Middle East. Its purpose was to provide the markets in India and the Middle East with the silk and luxury goods made in China. Spices, ointments, and silk were shipped from ports in India to the Roman Empire. In return, Rome sent gold coin, wines from Greece, and other goods not available in India. The Buddhism of the Kushan Empire spread into China because of the Silk Road, and many statues of the Buddha were carved using sculpture of Greek and Roman gods as models.

WRITING ACTIVITY:

Create an advertisement to publicize the opening of the Silk Road. The ad should persuade businessmen in Rome, the Middle East, India, and China of the benefits of using the new route.

TO ASSIST YOU:

- Research ads.
- Research the Silk Road.
- Research trade at the time of the Silk Road.
- Find out about travel during the time period.

Write a Classified Ad...

You are a trader and you need a manager for controlling your next shipment of Chinese goods from India to Rome.

Write a classified ad for this position.

On this page, begin a draft for your classified ad.

_____

_____

_____

_____

_____

_____

_____

_____

_____

_____

_____

_____

Share your draft with a partner. Make changes based upon suggestions. Proofread very carefully.

On a separate sheet of paper, write the final copy of your classified ad.

AUSTRALIAN ABORIGINES

BACKGROUND:

Land bridges existed between the Australian continent, New Guinea, and the Asian mainland. About 25,000 years ago the Aborigines began to arrive in Australia by way of the land bridges. The Australian Aborigines were a nomadic hunting people with no knowledge of domesticating animals or farming practices. By 1806, soldiers drove the Aborigines out of colonized regions. Native Australians were pushed back into the Australian interior, hunted and killed like kangaroos, introduced to liquor, given poisonous food, and encouraged to fight among themselves. Today, social and political conditions for the Aborigines are much the same.

WRITING ACTIVITY:

Write a dialogue between an Australian Aborigine and a Native American spokesperson in which they compare their social and political statuses in their respective countries.

TO ASSIST YOU:

• Research social and political conditions of Australian Aborigines and Native Americans.
• Identify the form and format for recording dialogue.
• Identify the focus/purpose of the dialogue.

Response for a TV Documentary...

You are the producer of a TV documentary on native peoples of the world.

You have a ten-minute time frame to present a response from the "majority" cultures to the dialogue between the Australian Aborigine and the Native American spokespersons.

Record the response.

On this page, begin a draft of the response.

_____

_____

_____

_____

_____

_____

_____

_____

_____

_____

_____

_____

_____

Share your draft with a partner. Make changes based upon suggestions. Proofread very carefully.

On a separate sheet of paper, write the final copy of the response based upon the dialogue.

AUSTRALIAN SETTLEMENT BY EUROPEANS

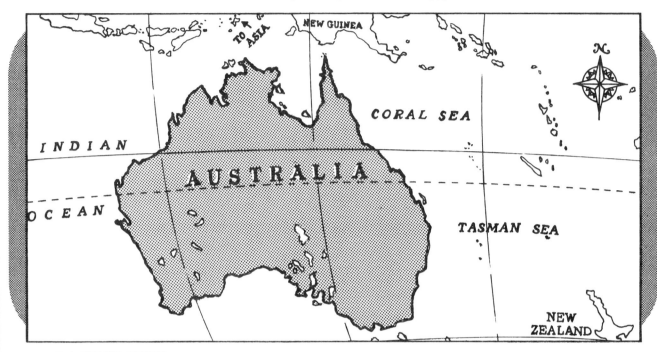

BACKGROUND:

Australia is a large island continent in the southern hemisphere. Though settled as early as 50,000 years ago by peoples from Asia via New Guinea, Australia was first sighted in 1606 by a Dutchman, William Jansz. After much confusion as to what exactly the land mass was, James Cook of Great Britain explored the fertile east coast and claimed the entire region in 1770. Cook named it New South Wales. Because of its remote location and the loss of the American colonies as reception sites for convicts, Britain, in 1787, began to send convicts to New South Wales. The first contingent arrived in Botany Bay on eleven ships on January 18, 1788. The relocation of convicts from Great Britain to eastern Australia ended in the early 1850s, but continued in western Australia until 1868. Over the period from 1787 to 1868, more than 160,000 convicts were sent to Australia. Today Australians who can trace their families to one of these convicts are considered to be very lucky and, because of their heritage, they are regarded as the first families of the country.

WRITING ACTIVITY:

As the descendant of one of the convicts relocated to Australia who has just recently discovered that relationship, write an article for *The Australian*. Your article should include background, historical information, and the impact and importance of your new-found relationship to the country.

TO ASSIST YOU:
• Find out about the role of convict-related individuals in modern-day Australia.
• Determine the social implication of the new information.

Make a Family Tree...

You are a descendant of one of the convicts relocated to Australia.

Compile a family tree to prove you are a member of one of the first families of Australia.

On this page, begin a draft of your family tree.

_____

_____

_____

_____

_____

_____

_____

_____

_____

_____

_____

_____

_____

_____

Share your draft with a partner. Make changes based upon suggestions. Proofread very carefully.

On a separate sheet of paper, write the final copy of your family tree.

ELIZABETH I OF ENGLAND

BACKGROUND:

Elizabeth I of England (1533-1603) ruled during a period which has been called the Golden Age, the British Renaissance, or simply, the Elizabethan Age. It was a time in which England became the first major non-Catholic country in western Europe to fight a major war with the Roman Catholic ones. England defeated the Spanish Armada to become the leading sea power of the time. England's seamen and traders became the leaders in their fields. The economy of England became extremely strong and stable, enabling the blossoming of art, literature, and music. The financial, military, political, and naval foundations were securely established to foster the creation of a world-wide empire controlled by Britain by the beginning of the nineteenth century.

WRITING ACTIVITY:

Write an essay to explain how and why a period in the history of a country or area might be named for an individual. Use Elizabeth I as the specific example to justify your general ideas.

TO ASSIST YOU:

• Find out about essays.
• Find out about syllogisms. (if then, therefore...)
• Find out about other figures who have given their names to eras.

Write an Essay...

You are yourself.

Propose a future time in history which will be identified with and named for you. Explain and justify how and why such a thing is going to happen.

On this page, begin a draft of your essay.

_____

_____

_____

_____

_____

_____

_____

_____

_____

_____

_____

_____

_____

Share your draft with a partner. Make changes based upon suggestions. Proofread very carefully.

On a separate sheet of paper, write the final copy of your essay based upon your projected contributions to history.

CATHERINE THE GREAT

BACKGROUND:
Catherine II, or Catherine the Great of Russia (1729-1796), was a German princess who, at the age of sixteen, was married to Czar Peter. Shortly after he became czar in 1762, Catherine and her cohorts deposed her husband, and he was later murdered. As czarina, Catherine attempted to bring Western influences in culture, science, and politics into Russia. She amassed a huge collection of Italian, French, and English art and even called for a legislative assembly to reform and modernize Russia's laws. While the legal reforms never happened and the ruling classes still were favored, Catherine did establish schools and hospitals, schooling for women, and more religious tolerance. She did not, however, do much for the vast majority of the Russian people. The serfs continued to be little more than possessions of the wealthy land owners.

WRITING ACTIVITY:
Write a fable about the life of Catherine II in the style of the Brothers Grimm. Be sure to include both the positive and dark sides of Catherine and her life.

TO ASSIST YOU:
• Find out about fables.
• Find out about Catherine's life.
• Find out about the Grimms' fairy tales.

Write a Fable...

Rewrite the fable about Catherine so that it can be the basis for a cartoon movie for children.

On this page begin a draft for your fable/screenplay.

_____

_____

_____

_____

_____

_____

_____

_____

_____

_____

_____

_____

_____

_____

Share your draft with a partner. Make changes based upon suggestions. Proofread very carefully.

On a separate sheet of paper, write the final copy of your fable/screenplay based upon Catherine's life.

STALIN

BACKGROUND:

Joseph Stalin (1879-1953) became the leader of the USSR (Union of Soviet Socialist Republics) after the death of Lenin in 1924. Through dictatorial power, Stalin transformed the Soviet Union into a Socialist state which became one of the world's great industrial and military powers; however, no one was allowed to oppose his personal rule. As a result, millions of people died under his brutal purges from 1935-1938 and again after World War II. His secret police terrorized the people. After World War II, Stalin's leadership was marked by the Cold War, during which he spread Communism to eleven other countries.

WRITING ACTIVITY:

Write an essay to explain how and why Stalin was a "legend in his own mind."

TO ASSIST YOU:

• Find out more about Stalin and his goals.
• Define: purge, dictator, Cold War, Communism, Socialism, Five Year Plan.
• Examine the results of Stalin's plans.

Write a Thesis Proposal...

As a contemporary historian, contradict the essay about Stalin's image of himself by explaining how and why the legend of Stalin could really be called a "nightmare."

Write a contradiction in the form of a thesis proposal.

On this page, begin a draft of your thesis proposal.

_____

_____

_____

_____

_____

_____

_____

_____

_____

_____

_____

_____

_____

Share your draft with a partner. Make changes based upon suggestions. Proofread very carefully.

On a separate sheet of paper, write the final copy of your thesis proposal based upon Stalin's essay.

WORLD WAR II

BACKGROUND:

World War II was fought from 1939 to 1945. The combatants, or opposing sides, were the Axis Powers and the Allies. The Axis side was made up of the countries of Germany, Italy, and Japan. The Allies consisted of most of the rest of the world's countries and the exiled French government. World War II was the first modern war to involve massive casualties in both the military and civilian populations. It is believed that more than 30 million people were killed and almost all the people of the earth were affected by the war. During the war, the Japanese won and later lost to the Allies much of China and most of Southeast Asia. The Germans and Italians won and also lost to the Allies almost all of continental Europe and large areas of north Africa. The war in Europe ended in May of 1945 after direct invasion and combat by the Allies. The war in Asia ended in August of 1945 after the detonation of two atomic bombs in Japan by the Allies.

WRITING ACTIVITY:

Plan, conduct, and document an interview with a participant in World War II.

TO ASSIST YOU:
• Find out about interviews and their structure.
• Determine the question and sequence for an interview.
• Find out the different kinds of roles of people involved in World War II.

Write a Summary...

You are the editor of a collection of World War II memoirs.

Edit and summarize your interview into one page.

On this page, begin a draft of your summary.

_____

_____

_____

_____

_____

_____

_____

_____

_____

_____

_____

_____

_____

Share your draft with a partner. Make changes based upon suggestions. Proofread very carefully.

On a separate sheet of paper, write the final copy based upon the interview.

THE HOLOCAUST

BACKGROUND:
The Holocaust, beginning in 1933 and ending in 1945, was an attempt by the Nazis to eliminate all people in Europe who did not fit their definition of "acceptable." This eventually included at least 11 million persons of many sub-groups of the cultures of Europe. Among these groups were Gypsies, Poles, Slavs, the physically or mentally handicapped, and Jews. Of all the persecuted groups, the Jews suffered the greatest loss. More than 6 million children, women, and men were systematically exterminated simply for being Jewish. This amounted to more than two-thirds of the Jewish population of Europe. People were gathered in concentration camps or ghettos and forced to work as slave labor for the Nazi war machine. When they became too weak or old or were too young to be productive, they were killed.

WRITING ACTIVITY:
Write a ballad that chronicles the Holocaust.

TO ASSIST YOU:
• Research the Holocaust.
• Research the elements of a ballad.

Write a Cover Letter...

You are a teacher. Your students have written works related to the Holocaust from their perspective.

Write a cover letter to the Director of the Holocaust Museum in Washington, D.C., in which you submit your students' works for inclusion in the permanent collection.

On this page, begin a draft of your cover letter.

_____

_____

_____

_____

_____

_____

_____

_____

_____

_____

_____

_____

_____

_____

Share your draft with a partner. Make changes based upon suggestions. Proofread very carefully.

On a separate sheet of paper, write the final copy of your cover letter.

THE UNITED NATIONS

Signing the United Nations charter

BACKGROUND:

The United Nations was founded on October 24, 1945, just after the ending of World War II. Its founding was based on the horror of the war and the belief that nations would work for world peace and security and the general betterment of all mankind. The charter was signed in June of 1945 by fifty countries, and to date more than 130 other countries have joined. Unlike its predecessor, the League of Nations, which was founded after World War I, the UN's founding membership included all of the major nations of the time. The UN headquarters is in New York City. The UN charter assigns four purposes: preserve world peace and security; encourage nations to be just toward each other; help nations cooperate to solve problems with each other; and serve as an agent to facilitate and encourage the first three goals. There are also seven principles: all members have equal rights; members will carry out duties under the charter; members will settle disputes peacefully; members will not use force or its threat against others except in self-defense; members will help the UN carry out the purposes of the charter; non-members have the same duty as members to preserve world peace and security; and the UN will not interfere in the actions of members taken within its own borders. Overriding all of this is the precept that any of these actions must not hurt other nations. The UN continues to do its work after fifty years.

WRITING ACTIVITY:

The Secretary General of the United Nations is really the overall head of the organization. Write a job description for the UN Secretary General.

TO ASSIST YOU:

• Research the process for becoming Secretary General of the UN.
• Research the requirements for the job of Secretary General.

Write a Response...

You are interested in the job of Secretary General of the United Nations.

Write a response.

On this page begin a draft of your response.

_____

_____

_____

_____

_____

_____

_____

_____

_____

_____

_____

_____

_____

_____

Share your draft with a partner. Make changes based upon suggestions. Proofread very carefully.

On a separate sheet of paper, write the final copy of your response for the job of Secretary General of the United Nations.

BIBLIOGRAPHY

This is a selected general-use bibliography. Specific bibliographic entries are available for each area of study.

Ahmed, I. *World Cultures, A Global Mosaic.* Englewood Cliffs: Prentice Hall, 1993.

Allen, Jack. *Americans.* New York: American Book Company, 1979.

Bacon, Phillip, Dr. *The United States, Its History and Neighbors.* Orlando: Harcourt Brace Jovanovich, 1991.

Bower, Bert. *Latin America and Canada.* Lexington: D.C. Heath and Company, 1987.

Compton's Encyclopedia. F.E. Compton, 1984.

Lind, L.R. *Ten Greek Plays.* Boston: Houghton Mifflin Company, 1957.

MacInnes, Colin. *Australia and New Zealand.* New York: Time Incorporated, 1968.

Merit Student's Encyclopedia. New York: Macmillan Educational Corp., 1978.

Perry, M. *Unfinished Journey.* Boston: Houghton Mifflin Company, 1983.

Webster's Seventh New Collegiate Dictionary. Massachusetts: G. & C. Merriam Co., 1961.

The World Book Encyclopedia. Chicago: Field Enterprises Educational Corp., 1986.

Worthy, W. *Black's Children's Encyclopedia.* London: Adam & Charles Black, 1961.